Christmas Treats

CRESCENT BOOKS

New York/Avenel, New Jersey

© Salamander Books Ltd 1992
129-137 York Way, London N7 9LG, United Kingdom

This 1992 edition published by Crescent Books, distributed
by Outlet Book Company, Inc., a Random House Company,
40 Englehard Avenue, Avenel, New Jersey 07001

Printed and bound in Belgium

ISBN 0-517-06958-X

87654321

All correspondence concerning the content of this volume
should be addressed to Salamander Books Ltd.

CREDITS

Recipes by: *Pat Alburey, Carole Handslip,
Lesley Mackley and Janice Murfitt*

Editor: *Lisa Dyer*

Photographer: *Steve Tanner*

Designer: *Louise Bruce*

Illustrator: *Pauline Bayne*

Filmset: *SX Composing Ltd*

Colour Separation: *P & W Graphics*

Contents

Advent Crescents

2 cups all-purpose flour
pinch of salt
½ cup sugar
1⅓ cups ground almonds
1 cup butter, cut into small cubes
3 egg yolks
few drops almond extract
confectioners' sugar to decorate

Begin by sifting flour and salt into a bowl, then mix in the sugar and ground almonds. Make a well in the center.

Place butter, egg yolks and almond extract in the center of the mixture. With fingertips, gently work butter with yolks, gradually incorporating flour, sugar and almonds until the mixture forms a soft dough. Wrap in plastic wrap and refrigerate for 30 minutes. Preheat oven to 350°F.

Divide dough into ½oz pieces, about the size of a walnut. Shape each piece into a thin roll, about 4in long. Curve around to form a crescent shape. Place on an ungreased cookie sheet and bake for 15 minutes until lightly browned. Allow to cool on the cookie sheets. Sift liberally with confectioners' sugar. Remove the crescents from the cookie sheets to a serving plate.

Makes 42

Cinnamon Fingers

2 egg whites
1¼ cups sugar
1 tablespoon plus 1 teaspoon potato flour
2 teaspoons ground cinnamon
1¼ cups ground almonds
⅓ cup shredded coconut

Preheat oven to 350°F. Grease several cookie sheets and line with waxed paper. In a bowl, whisk egg whites until stiff. Sift sugar, potato flour and cinnamon into the bowl. Add ground almonds.

Mix gently together to form a stiff paste. Put into a pastry bag, fitted with a ⅜in plain nozzle and pipe 3in lengths of mixture on cookie sheets, spaced well apart. Sprinkle evenly with coconut.

Bake for 25 minutes until lightly browned. Allow to cool on cookie sheets for a few minutes, then remove to wire racks to cool completely.

Makes 40

Florentines

¼ cup unsalted butter
⅓ cup heavy whipping cream
½ cup soft light-brown sugar
finely grated peel of 1 large lemon
2 teaspoons lemon juice
¼ cup all-purpose flour, sifted
½ cup blanched almonds, slivered
½ cup chopped mixed citrus peel
⅓ cup chopped glacé cherries
2 tablespoons raisins
3 tablespoons chopped dried apricots
2 tablespoons chopped angelica
6oz semi-sweet chocolate, broken in pieces

Preheat oven to 350°F. Grease several large cookie sheets and line with waxed paper. Put butter, cream, sugar, lemon peel and juice into a large saucepan and stir over a moderate heat until melted. Remove from heat and stir in flour, nuts, citrus peel, fruit and angelica. Drop teaspoonfuls on cookie sheets. Using a fork dipped in cold water, flatten each mound to a circle about 2½in in diameter.

Bake for 10-12 minutes until lightly browned around the edges. Let cool for a few minutes, then transfer to wire racks to cool completely. Melt chocolate in a double boiler or in a small bowl placed over a pan of hot water. Spread the flat side of each florentine with chocolate. Using a fork, make wavy lines into the chocolate. Place on a cookie sheet, chocolate side uppermost, and leave to set.

Makes 28

Sugar & Spice Cookies

2 cups all-purpose flour
pinch of salt
½ teaspoon ground cinnamon
¼ teaspoon ground allspice
¼ teaspoon ground mace
¼ teaspoon ground cloves
½ teaspoon baking powder
½ cup sugar
½ cup butter
1 egg, beaten

GLAZE:
1 small egg, beaten
1 tablespoon milk
2 teaspoons superfine sugar
2 tablespoons granulated sugar

Grease several cookie sheets. Sift flour, salt, spices, baking powder and sugar into a bowl. Cut-in butter until mixture resembles fine bread crumbs. Stir in egg and mix by hand to form a soft dough. Roll out dough to ⅛in thick. Cut out shapes using cookie cutters. Place on cookie sheets. Re-knead and re-roll trimmings and cut out again to make 32 in total. Refrigerate shapes for 30 minutes. Preheat oven to 350°F.

To make the glaze, stir together egg, milk and superfine sugar. Brush glaze over each cookie, then sprinkle with half the granulated sugar. Bake for 15-20 minutes. Remove and immediately sprinkle with remaining sugar. Carefully remove cookies from sheets to wire racks to cool.

Makes 32

15

Tiny Chocolate Logs

3 eggs
2 tablespoons plus 2 teaspoons sugar
¼ cup all-purpose flour
1 tablespoon cocoa powder

FILLING AND DECORATION:
1¼ cups heavy whipping cream
4oz semi-sweet chocolate, broken in pieces
marzipan toadstools

Prehat oven to 400°F. Line a 12in baking sheet (1in deep) with waxed paper. Place eggs and sugar in a bowl set over a saucepan of simmering water and whisk until thick and pale.

Remove bowl, and continue whisking until the mixture leaves a trail when the whisk is lifted. Sift flour and cocoa on the surface of the mixture and gently fold in. Pour on to the prepared baking sheet and spread to the edges. Bake for 8-10 minutes, or until firm to the touch. Cool, then turn out and remove paper. Trim edges and cut in half lengthwise. Place ¼ cup whipping cream in a bowl with the chocolate. Place over a pan of hot water and stir until melted. Whip remaining cream until almost thick.

When chocolate has cooled, fold it carefully into the whipped cream. Spread one-third of the chocolate cream over each strip of the sponge cake. Firmly roll each strip from the long edge. Wrap in plastic wrap and chill until firm. Cut each roll into 6 lengths, spread with remaining chocolate and mark lines. Decorate with marzipan. Keep cool until ready to serve.

Makes 12

Harptree
Cookies

¾ cup unsalted butter
½ cup confectioners' sugar, sifted
finely grated peel of 1 lemon
1¾ cups all-purpose flour
pinch of salt

TO DECORATE:
5-6 glacé cherries, cut into small pieces
80 small angelica 'leaves'
confectioners' sugar for sifting

In a bowl, beat butter with confectioners' sugar until light and fluffy, then beat in lemon peel.

Sift the flour and salt into the bowl and work by hand to form a soft dough. On a floured surface, knead lightly until smooth, then shape into a thick roll, about 12in long. Wrap in plastic wrap and refrigerate for 4-5 hours or overnight. Preheat oven to 350°F. Grease several cookie sheets.

Cutting diagonally, cut chilled dough into thin slices, about ¼in thick. Place on cookie sheets. If desired, decorate each cookie with cherry and angelica pieces. Bake for 15-20 minutes until just slightly browned. Allow to cool on cookie sheets for a few minutes, then remove to wire racks to cool completely. When cold, sift lightly with confectioners' sugar.

Makes 40

Egg Nog Brownies

2 eggs
1 tablespoon brandy
few drops vanilla
½ cup butter
4oz semi-sweet chocolate, broken in pieces
1 cup superfine sugar
1⅓ cups soft light-brown sugar
1¼ cups all-purpose flour
1 cup chopped pecan nuts

Grease a shallow pan measuring about 11 × 7 × 1¼in. Line base with waxed paper. Preheat oven to 350°F.

In a bowl, lightly whisk eggs with brandy and vanilla. Put butter and chocolate into a large saucepan and place over a moderate heat. Stir continuously until melted. Remove from heat. Stir in superfine and brown sugar, then egg mixture, flour and pecans. Pour into prepared pan and spread evenly. Bake for 30 minutes or until a cocktail stick inserted into the center comes out clean.

Allow brownie mixture to cool in pan. When cool, cut into 24 small squares: cut evenly into 4 lengthwise and 6 widthwise. Remove from the pan with a small knife. Brownies keep well for up to one week if stored in an airtight container, in a cool place.

Makes 24

Festive Rings

2 cups all-purpose flour
½ teaspoon superfine sugar
½ teaspoon salt
1 tablespoon butter
1 teaspoon active dry yeast
½ cup warm water
1 egg yolk, to glaze
red and green food colorings
colored ribbon

In a bowl, put sifted flour, sugar and salt. Cut-in butter finely. Stir in yeast and enough warm water to form a soft dough. Knead on a lightly floured surface until smooth and no longer sticky.

Return dough to bowl, cover with plastic wrap and leave for 5 minutes. Re-knead dough until smooth. Cut off one-quarter of the dough and reserve. Shape remainder into a 24in roll. Cut in half and shape into 2 rings by joining ends together. Place on a floured cookie sheet. Cover and leave in a warm place to rise for 20-30 minutes. Meanwhile, roll out remaining dough thinly and cut out 40 holly leaves. Shape 40 beads of dough into berries. Put on a floured plate, cover with plastic wrap and refrigerate.

Preheat oven to 425°F. Divide egg yolk between 3 egg cups. Add 1 teaspoon of water to one and brush over dough rings. Add red and green food coloring separately to remaining cups. Bake rings for 10-15 minutes until risen, but pale. Arrange leaves and berries on rings, then glaze leaves green and berries red. Bake again for 5-6 minutes. Decorate with ribbon.

Makes 2

Christmas Shortbread

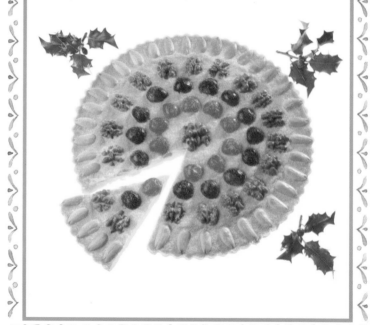

$1\sfrac{3}{4}$ *cups all-purpose flour*
pinch of salt
3 tablespoons cornstarch
$\sfrac{1}{4}$ *cup superfine sugar*
1 cup butter

TO DECORATE:
about 37 blanched almonds
about 19 walnut halves
7 green glacé cherries, cut into halves
5 red glacé cherries, cut into halves
superfine sugar for sprinkling

Sift flour, salt and cornstarch into a bowl, then add sugar. Cut-in butter until the mixture forms coarse crumbs. Gently work mixture together to form a soft dough. On a floured surface, roll out dough to a little smaller than a 10in circle. Place dough in a 10in fluted pie pan with removable bottom, and press out gently to fit pan exactly, pressing well into the flutes. Smooth surface with the back of a spoon. Prick well with a fork.

To decorate shortbread, arrange almonds in a neat ring around the edge of the dough. Add a ring of walnut halves, then a ring of green cherries followed by red cherries. Place a walnut half in the center. Refrigerate for 30 minutes. Preheat oven to 350°F. Bake shortbread for 45-50 minutes until lightly browned. Cool in the pan. Sift lightly with superfine sugar. Carefully remove from pan to a serving plate.

Serves 16

Brandied
Mincemeat

6 cups raisins
3⅓ cups currants
1 cup dried apricots
¾ cup dates
1 cup candied peel
¾ cup whole almonds
1lb cooking apples, peeled and cored
finely grated peel and juice of 2 lemons
2¼ cups soft light-brown sugar
1 cup unsalted butter, melted
1 tablespoon ground mixed spice
⅔ cup brandy

In a bowl, put raisins and currants. Then chop or mince apricots, dates, candied peel, almonds and apples. Add to the bowl with lemon peel and juice, and mix together well. Stir in sugar, butter, mixed spice and brandy. Stir the mixture until evenly blended. Cover bowl with plastic wrap and refrigerate for 2 days.

Preheat oven to 400°F. Sterilize six 1-pint jam jars and lids, and keep warm. Stir mincemeat thoroughly, then spoon into hot jars, filling each to the top. Cover each with paraffin and seal with lids. Label clearly and store in a cool dry place for up to 6 months.

Makes 6 jars

27

Mince Pies

3 cups all-purpose flour
3/4 cup butter
2 tablespoons superfine sugar
1 egg, separated
1½ cups mincemeat (see page 27)
red and green food coloring

Preheat oven to 400°F. Sift flour into a bowl. Cut-in butter finely with the fingers until the mixture resembles bread crumbs. Using a fork, stir in sugar, egg yolk and enough cold water to mix to a soft dough. Knead gently on a lightly floured surface.

Roll out pastry thinly and cut out twenty 3in circles and twenty 2in circles. Line 20 miniature tart pans with the larger pastry circles, prick the base of each with a fork, and half-fill with mincemeat. Brush edges of each pastry lid with water, invert and press on top of tart to seal edges. Pierce a hole in the center of each lid to allow steam to escape. Roll out pastry trimmings thinly and, using a holly leaf cutter, cut out 40 holly leaves and mark leaf veins with a knife. Roll tiny balls of pastry to form berries.

Brush each miniature tart top with egg white and arrange holly leaves and berries on top. Bake for 15 minutes until cooked, but pale. Divide remaining egg white between 2 cups; color one red and the other green with food coloring. Brush leaves with green glaze and berries with red. Bake for a further 5 minutes. Cool on a wire rack.

Makes 20

Brandy Butter

1 cup unsalted butter
1 cup superfine sugar
⅓ cup brandy
holly sprig, to decorate

Put butter in a bowl or food processor fitted with a metal blade. Beat or process butter until white and creamy. Add sugar and beat or process until light and fluffy.

Add brandy, a drop at a time, beating continuously until enough has been added to well-flavor the butter. Take care the mixture does not curdle through over-beating.

Pile butter into a glass dish and serve with a spoon, or, if preferred, spread the mixture about ½in thick over a flat dish and chill until hard. Using a fancy cutter, cut the butter into shapes and arrange in a serving dish. Decorate with holly. Serve the butter with holiday desserts, such as mince pies or fruit cake served warm from the oven.

Serves 8

Southern Comfort Cakes

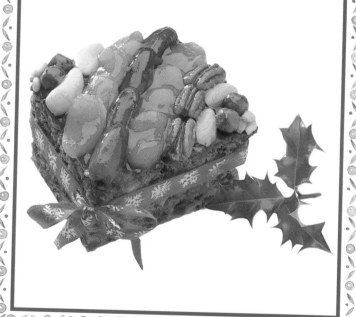

1¼ cups butter
½ cup plus 2 tablespoons light corn syrup
1¼ cups Southern Comfort
finely grated peel and juice of 1 orange and 1 lemon
6¼ cups mixed dried fruit
2½ cups chopped dried apricots
2¼ cups chopped dried dates
¾ teaspoon baking soda
3 eggs
3½ cups whole-wheat self-rising flour
2 teaspoons ground allspice
½ cup apricot jam
2¼ cups assorted nuts
apricots and dates to decorate

Preheat oven to 300°F. Grease and double-line a 10 × 8 × 2in baking pan with waxed paper. Place pan on a double-waxed-paper-lined cookie sheet. In a large saucepan, place butter, corn syrup, Southern Comfort, citrus peels and juices. Heat until almost boiling. Add mixed fruit, apricots and dates; stir until well-blended and leave until almost cold. Stir in baking soda, eggs, flour and allspice.

Spoon mixture into pan, and level top. Bake for 2¼-2½ hours. Cool in the pan, then invert and wrap in foil until required. Boil and sieve apricot jam. Cut cake into 6 pieces, brush with apricot jam, then arrange nuts and fruit over top. Glaze with remaining jam. Leave until set, then wrap in plastic wrap and tie with ribbon.

Makes 6

Glacé Fruit Cake

2½ cups chopped mixed glacé fruit
1 cup chopped dried apricots
1 cup chopped pecans
finely grated peel and juice of 1 lemon
3 cups all-purpose flour
1 teaspoon baking powder
1½ teaspoons ground mixed spice
1⅔ cups ground almonds
1¾ cups superfine sugar
1½ cups butter, softened
4 eggs

TOPPING:
¼ cup apricot jam
mixed glacé fruit and nuts

Line an 8in square cake pan with double-thickness, greased, waxed paper, extending waxed paper above edges of pan. Place pan on a cookie sheet lined with a double-thickness of waxed paper. Preheat oven to 275°F. Mix together first four ingredients. Then sift flour, baking powder and mixed spice into a bowl, and add almonds, sugar, butter and eggs. Mix, then beat for 2 minutes. Stir in fruit and nut mixture.

Put mixture in the pan and smooth the top. Bake for 2¼-2½ hours. Cool in pan, invert, and wrap in foil. Place jam and 2 teaspoons water in a pan, bring to the boil, stirring, and sieve. Brush the top of the cake with the jam glaze. Arrange fruit and nuts on top, and brush with remaining glaze. Leave to set. Decorate with ribbon and holly, if desired.

Serves 30

Cranberry Nut Cake

TOPPING:
¼ cup unsalted butter
½ cup granulated sugar
2¼ cups cranberries
½ cup roughly chopped pecan nuts

CAKE:
3 eggs
⅓ cup superfine sugar
⅔ cup self-rising flour
2 tablespoons cocoa powder
pinch of baking powder
½ teaspoon ground cinnamon
3 tablespoons unsalted butter, melted

Preheat oven to 350°F. Place a cookie sheet in the oven. For the topping, spread butter over the base and sides of a deep 9in round cake pan. Coat with granulated sugar. In a bowl, mix together cranberries and pecans and spread evenly over the base of the cake pan.

For the cake, set a bowl over a pan of hot, but not boiling, water. Place eggs and superfine sugar in bowl and whisk until thick and light, and the whisk leaves a trail when lifted out of mixture. Sift flour, cocoa, baking powder and cinnamon into the mixture, a little at a time, folding in carefully each time. Fold in melted butter.

Pour mixture over topping mixture. Place pan on the heated cookie sheet and bake for 40 minutes or until cake is firm and a skewer inserted in the center comes out clean. Leave cake to cool in pan for 10 minutes. Then invert on to a plate, and cut into wedges to serve.

Serves 6-8

Plum & Apple Tart

1 6oz package pizza crust mix
warm water
2 tablespoons butter, melted
¾ cup ground almonds
¼ cup superfine sugar
1 teaspoon ground mixed spice
1lb cooking apples, peeled, cored and sliced
2lbs plums, pitted and halved
⅓ cup plum jam, boiled and sieved
1 tablespoon flaked almonds

Preheat oven to 425°F. Place pizza mix in a bowl. Add warm water according to instructions on package. Knead dough until smooth; cover and leave for 5 minutes. Re-knead dough and roll out to a 2in round on a lightly floured surface. Place in a greased 10in pie pan, and brush dough with butter. In a bowl, mix together ground almonds, sugar and mixed spice. Sprinkle over the dough.

Arrange apple slices and plum halves neatly over almond mixture. Bake for 20-30 minutes until dough is well risen and filling is tender. Cool on a wire rack. Then brush with plum jam to glaze, and sprinkle with flaked almonds.

Serves 12

Hot Chocolate Drinks

1oz semi-sweet chocolate, grated
1¼ cups hot black coffee
2 teaspoons soft dark-brown sugar
1 tablespoon dark rum
2 tablespoons heavy whipping cream, whipped

COFFEE CALYPSO:
4 tablespoons dark crème de cacao
2 teaspoons dark-brown sugar
1 cup hot black coffee
4 tablespoons heavy cream
instant coffee granules

HOT CHOCOLATE NOG:
3oz semi-sweet chocolate, chopped
1¾ cups hot milk
1 tablespoon superfine sugar
1 egg
3 tablespoons brandy

For Mexicanas, blend chocolate, coffee and sugar in a blender or food processor. Add rum and pour into 2 heatproof glasses. Top with whipped cream and serve immediately.

For Coffee Calypso, halve all ingredients. Pour crème de cacao into 2 heatproof glasses, then add sugar and coffee. Stir well, then slowly pour cream over the back of a teaspoon into each glass so it floats on top. Sprinkle with coffee granules and serve.

For Hot Chocolate Nog, blend chocolate, hot milk and sugar in a blender or food processor until chocolate has melted. Add egg and brandy and blend for 20 seconds. Pour into 2 heatproof glasses and serve immediately.

Each recipe serves 2

Christmas Eve Mull

1 bottle white wine
1 bottle red wine
1¼ cup sweet red vermouth
1 tablespoon Angostura bitters
6 strips orange peel
8 whole cloves
1 cinnamon stick
8 cardamom pods, crushed
1 tablespoon dark raisins
½ cup superfine sugar
lemon, lime, orange and apple slices, to decorate

Pour white and red wines into a large stainless steel or enamel saucepan. Add vermouth, bitters, orange peel, cloves, cinnamon and cardamom pods. Heat wine mixture gently until very hot, but do not boil. Remove saucepan from heat, cover with a lid and allow to cool. Strain wine into a bowl.

Just before serving, return wine to a clean saucepan, add raisins and sugar. Heat gently until sugar has dissolved and wine is hot enough to drink. Decorate with fruit slices and serve in heatproof glasses or mugs.

Serves 18

Hot Buttered Rum

4 cinnamon sticks
1 tablespoon plus 1 teaspoon soft light-brown sugar
½ cup dark rum
2½ cups apple cider
2 tablespoons butter
1 teaspoon mace
4 lemon slices

Divide cinnamon sticks, sugar and rum between 4 warm heat-proof glasses or mugs.

Place apple cider in a saucepan and heat until very hot, but not boiling. Fill each glass or mug almost to the top with the cider. Add a knob of butter, a sprinkling of mace and a lemon slice to each glass or mug. Stir well and serve hot.

Serves 4